19.95po

||||| |||||||||||||||||||||||||||||
W9-CCD-145

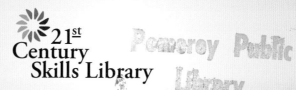

21st Century Skills Library

COOL STEM CAREERS

TRANSPORTATION PLANNER

NEL YOMTOV

Published in the United States of America by
Cherry Lake Publishing, Ann Arbor, Michigan
www.cherrylakepublishing.com

Content Adviser
Joe Grengs, PhD, AICP, Associate Professor, Urban and Regional Planning, University
of Michigan, Ann Arbor, Michigan

Photo Credits: Cover and page 1, ©CandyBox Images/Shutterstock, Inc.;
page 4, ©SeanPavonePhoto/Shutterstock, Inc.; page 6, ©Blazej Lyjak/
Shutterstock, Inc.; page 8, ©Paul Matthew Photography/Shutterstock, Inc.;
page 10, ©TonyV3112/Shutterstock, Inc.; page 12, ©Norman Pogson/Shuttestock,
Inc.; page 15, ©Andrew Barker/Shutterstock, Inc.; page 16, ©Goodluz/Shutterstock,
Inc.; page 18, ©Henryk Sadura/Shutterstock, Inc.; page 20, ©Robert Kneschke/
Shutterstock, Inc.; page 23, ©Nickolay Vinokurov/Shutterstock, Inc.; page 24,
©Jorg Hackemann/Shutterstock, Inc.; page 25, ©StockLite/Shutterstock, Inc.

Library of Congress Cataloging-in-Publication Data
Yomtov, Nelson.
    Transportation planner/Nel Yomtov.
        p. cm.—(Cool STEM careers) (21st century skills library)
    Audience: Grades 4–6.
    Includes bibliographical references and index.
    ISBN 978-1-62431-008-9 (lib. bdg.) — ISBN 978-1-62431-032-4 (pbk.) —
ISBN 978-1-62431-056-0 (e-book)
    1. Transportation—Vocational guidance—Juvenile literature. 2. Transportation—
Planning—Juvenile literature. 3. City planners—Juvenile literature. 4. Vocational
guidance—Juvenile literature. I. Title.
    HE152.Y65 2013
    711'.7023—dc23   2012034737

Cherry Lake Publishing would like to acknowledge
the work of The Partnership for 21st Century Skills.
Please visit *www.21stcenturyskills.org* for more information.

Printed in the United States of America
Corporate Graphics Inc.
January 2013
CLSP12

TABLE OF CONTENTS

CHAPTER ONE
A MOVING EXPERIENCE

Nathalie and her mother were visiting New York City for the first time. As they walked along the

Taxis and buses are among the ways to get around large cities such as New York.

busy streets, Nathalie said, "I've never seen so many cars and trucks and buses and taxis in my life!"

"Don't forget the airplane that took us here and the subway we're about to get on," said Nathalie's mom. "And all the people walking, too!"

"There are so many ways to get around the city," Nathalie said. "Yet it doesn't seem at all confusing."

"That's because the city's system of **transportation** is carefully worked out," replied Nathalie's mom. "It takes lots of planning to move people and things from place to place."

"That sounds like something I'd like to do," said Nathalie. "Imagine being responsible for helping an entire city be on the move!"

⬛ ⬛ ⬛

Transportation is the business of moving people and goods from place to place. It involves road, air, rail, and water travel. It even includes traveling on foot. Have you ever wondered, for instance, how many different ways there are for people to get to their jobs? Some travel on a subway or a commuter railroad. Some drive or **carpool**. A few bicycle to work. Others live close enough to walk.

Moving goods is another part of the field of transportation. **Freight** is most often transported by train, airplane, truck, or ship. To transport goods efficiently, a large city or region must have a system of railways, airports, roads, and ports. Moving people and goods in and out of cities affects the quality of people's lives. Well-organized transportation systems make it easier for people to get from place to place. This makes a city more appealing to live in or visit.

The trained professionals who develop transportation plans and programs are called transportation planners. They carefully study the transportation needs for an area. This includes anything from large cities with millions of people to

Bicycle lanes keep cyclists and drivers from getting in each other's way.

small towns and villages with only a few dozen homes. Planners determine if additional transportation facilities are needed and where they should be built. Planners suggest a range of transportation options. They might recommend roads, public **transit** routes, or bike lanes.

Transportation planning is a critical part of a larger field known as city, or **urban**, planning. Urban planners manage a community's growth and change. They also work to protect the environment and preserve its historic buildings and neighborhoods.

LIFE & CAREER SKILLS

During the 2010s, Nat Bottigheimer was a planner at the Washington Metropolitan Area Transit Authority in Washington, D.C. He oversaw a program that included new bus services and parking services at transit stations. Why did planning interest Bottigheimer? "I was immediately captivated by all the things that I remembered about spending three years in England growing up. I loved the buses. I loved the trains. I loved being on public transit and being with people. And I loved the urban settings associated with transit and people."

The origins of city planning date back to ancient civilizations, including those of Greece and China. Evidence shows that these groups planned the layout of their roads and the growth of their towns. From about 500 BCE, the Romans had complex networks of paved streets. These were used to transport people and goods throughout their entire empire. In the 1800s, the development of the steam engine led to the birth

Airplanes can quickly deliver cargo all around the world.

of steam-powered railways in Europe and the United States. People and freight could travel faster and farther than ever before.

The early 20th century saw the biggest growth in transportation planning. Millions of motorized vehicles appeared in the United States and other countries. Cities of all sizes began to construct or improve streets to accommodate them. Vast, interconnected networks of paved roadways were built. This made the transport of people and freight easier and quicker.

The development of the airplane in the 1920s gave people a fast new way to travel. It also gave industries a speedier shipping option. Throughout the world, airports were built to handle the ever-increasing numbers of passengers and freight flying each year. Of course, transportation systems to and from the airports had to be designed and built to get people—and goods—to the runways.

Transportation planners keep cities and nations on the go. They organize important projects that work to fulfill everyone's transportation needs.

CHAPTER TWO
ON THE JOB

I t is a transportation planner's job to study the present and future transportation needs of a community. Transportation planners consider all of an area's possible forms of transportation. They determine the costs of various improvements and

Transportation planners carefully analyze traffic patterns to find ways of reducing congestion on roads.

ensure that any plan is accessible to all people, including those with disabilities. Then they work with others to develop plans and programs that will have a positive impact on the environment, the community, and the individual residents. Successful planners let interested groups be part of the decision-making process while they evaluate options.

Consider an example. An urban area has congested, or very heavy, traffic at a certain time of day. A transportation planner is called on to help solve the problem. The first step is to collect and analyze information about the problem. What is causing all the traffic? Has the community already tried any solutions that failed? Are construction projects on the road causing delays? Might the congestion be caused by heavy traffic at nearby shopping areas or sports arenas? Have drivers been urged to use other forms of transportation, such as bikes, public transit, and walking?

To gather this information, transportation planners might design surveys and questionnaires for the people affected by the congestion, such as city officials, drivers, or local merchants. They might also conduct interviews in person. Planners analyze this data using computer software to understand the problem more clearly and identify possible solutions. Some of the time, they develop original ideas for solving the problem. Other times, they find solutions that have been successful in other places.

The next important step is to predict the impact, or effect, of each proposal. Planners work with land developers, engineers, planning boards, citizens' groups, agencies, and other organizations. Together, they estimate the social, economic, and environmental effects of their proposals. Whether it is a highway, transit, or **aviation** project, the transportation planner must ask many questions. Will homes have to be torn

Transportation planners oversee the construction of new highways.

down to build new roads? Will construction or changes in the traffic or movement of **pedestrians** harm local businesses? How will construction affect the environment? Have all regulations been followed?

LEARNING & INNOVATION SKILLS

One way to understand transportation planning is to learn the history of planning in the United States. Make your own timeline by reading about the development of transportation. You can begin with travel by horse and riverboat in the 18th century. Then research the toll roads and canals built in the early 19th century. Learn about the rapid expansion of railroads, the arrival of trolley cars and automobiles, the birth of interstate highways, and the network of airports throughout the country. The history of moving people and goods from place to place is a fascinating story. It will make you wonder what the future holds.

When planners are ready to propose their recommendations for transportation improvements or projects, they meet with elected officials and the public. At these meetings, planners explain their ideas. They also hear the views of the people affected by the proposed projects. Concerned officials and citizens may object to the cost of the project or its impact on the community. Planners often revise or even abandon projects after gathering new information. Input from various officials and the public provides valuable information that planners can use to improve their proposals and eventually win support.

21ST CENTURY CONTENT

Taking public transportation to John F. Kennedy (JFK) Airport in New York City has always been a challenge. But transportation planners offered a solution: build a **monorail** connecting the airport terminals with the Long Island Rail Road commuter rail system and the city's subway lines. Government and airport officials liked the idea. They got the support of local residents, set aside the funds, and built the monorail. It opened in 2003, though on a much smaller scale than originally planned. Every day, thousands of people ride AirTrain JFK.

Tens of thousands of airplanes take off and land around the world every day.

A typical day for a transportation planner usually includes office meetings and site visits. Analyzing information, such as environmental impact or the effects of governmental regulations on transportation issues, is also part of the normal workday. Planners must prepare reports, draft budgets, and produce various documents to obtain project

Transportation planners often work with architects during construction projects.

approvals. Transportation planning, however, isn't all about analyzing and preparing reports. A large part of a planner's day often involves talking with other people, sharing information, and working on solutions as part of a team.

A transportation planner might be involved in a wide range of projects. One day, a planner might determine where the new stops on a subway or bus expansion should be located. Another day might be devoted to planning for the location of a new airport. At the same time, a planner might be working with architects and artists to build miniature cities. The **models** they create help demonstrate transportation ideas. Or a planner might use **computer simulations** to show how new roads will be built and how they will improve traffic.

Most planners work regular 40-hour weeks. But a planner might also attend one or two evening or weekend meetings per week. These meetings are usually held with city officials or the public. The people discuss new development proposals. Planners sometimes face opposition to their proposals. Decisions can be delayed by weeks, months, or even years of debate. Planners who enjoy playing a role in shaping cities should have the patience to "go with the flow" and learn to work cooperatively with different groups to address a variety of needs.

CHAPTER THREE
GETTING THE RIGHT EDUCATION

Transportation planners require a mix of skills to design or improve transportation systems. Planners need strong communication skills. They are frequently required to

GPS technology provides planners with detailed, precise measurements.

write reports and deliver oral presentations. They may speak with city officials, citizens, or experts in many fields. Therefore, the ability to convey information effectively and accurately to a broad range of people is essential.

Planners also need to have solid research skills. Knowing how to gather and analyze data is especially important. Incorrect or incomplete data analysis can lead to inaccurate conclusions. This could doom the success of a project. Once the data is gathered, planners need to use critical thinking and problem solving to identify the strengths and weaknesses of their solutions. They must develop alternatives if needed.

An ability to work with numbers is required for transportation planners. Knowledge of arithmetic, algebra, geometry, and statistics is a necessary part of the job. Every day, planners work with numbers. They might study the number of cars traveling on a highway or of transit passengers during rush hour. They may look at the amount of raw material being transported on a ship, the number of miles of railroad track, and much more.

Being able to use new computer-based technologies is another critical skill. Planners need to have the skills to use sophisticated data collection and analysis techniques. Global Positioning Systems (GPS) and Geographic Information Systems (GIS) are examples. Planners also use software that creates models to predict the impact of new facilities and services. To help determine costs and develop budgets, planners must use the latest accounting programs. Knowing economic and accounting practices, finance, and banking helps a planner better analyze and report critical financial data.

Putting yourself on the path toward being a planner begins with the right education. You will need at least a bachelor's degree. Most planners also hold a master's degree. Statistics show that a master's degree can help a planner earn about $3,000 to $8,000 more per year.

All transportation planners need college degrees.

The professional degree in planning is called a master of urban planning (MUP) or a master of city planning (MCP). Many master degree programs offer specializations, such as transportation planning. Other types of urban or city planners include housing and development planners, historic preservation planners, and health and social service planners. Because of the broad range of planning jobs, once you obtain your degree, you can become involved with transportation planning in a variety of ways. Many transportation planners start their careers by working in civil engineering, architecture, or public administration. Public administration deals with city management.

Most MUP or MCP programs take two years to complete. They often require students to serve internships with planning departments in government or private firms. Internships provide students valuable work experience. They may help lead to employment after graduation.

Students of transportation planning may take classes in a variety of subjects. These include environmental studies, economics, geography, statistics, and computer programming. Political science classes might help students understand the role of government in creating transportation solutions. Art and design courses teach the skills to think visually about the systems and facilities that students will be designing after graduation.

Attending college or university may be years away. Still, it is not too early for future planners to learn how they can become involved. Middle school students might be able to find a summer or after-school program in urban planning. You can also check to see if any organizations or businesses in your area run competitions that encourage students to learn about planning needs and careers in planning. Your school might even run a program that features educational field trips and classes that focus on urban planning. It's all worth checking out.

Planners need to think carefully about the visual designs of their projects.

CHAPTER FOUR
YOUR FUTURE AS A TRANSPORTATION PLANNER

The field of transportation planning is growing even faster than the broader field of urban planning. One reason

Subway trains provide people who live in major cities with a convenient alternative to driving.

for this is the need to find alternatives to cars. Public transit systems also face funding challenges.

Ever-increasing car usage causes traffic congestion, longer traveling times, and air pollution. As gasoline prices continue to rise, government officials will be turning to transportation planners. Planners work to develop improved transportation systems and facilities. They also try to find innovative ways to encourage residents to walk, bike, or use public transit instead of driving.

In many large U.S. cities, public transit systems are facing overwhelming obstacles. Some of the systems are more than 100 years old. They are costly to operate and repair. Many cities have been forced to raise fares and cut services. Saving money by eliminating bus routes in less-populated areas is not uncommon, for example. Bridges and tunnels are often in disrepair, having been neglected for decades. Here, too, transportation planners are needed to find solutions.

In times of economic decline, such as the worldwide economic crisis that began in 2008, many projects that require planners are postponed or canceled. With less tax revenue, a city often has to decrease its budget. This means it hires fewer people. Local governments tend to lay off workers less frequently than private industry, however. Even in the **private sector**, firms rely on their planners to generate work for their engineering or construction divisions. In this case, planners are most likely to ride out the hard times and remain employed.

Most transportation planners work for the government. They may work for a town, county, or city government. Some planners work for a regional planning agency. They organize projects covering entire metropolitan areas. Others work for state or federal agencies. These agencies include the National Park Service, the Department of Transportation, and the Environmental Protection Agency.

The U.S. Bureau of Labor Statistics does not separate the different specialties within planning. As of 2010, about 40,300

A transportation planner's job is challenging, yet rewarding.

urban and regional planners worked in the United States. State and local governments employed about 75 percent of them. Roughly 14 percent worked for private architectural or engineering businesses. About 6 percent worked in private scientific and technical services.

As of May 2010, the yearly median salary for urban and regional planners was $63,000. The median salary is the wage that half the workers earned more than and half earned less than. The lowest 10 percent of planners earned less than $40,400. The top 10 percent earned more than $96,400.

Planners working for local and state governments earned less than planners working for private companies. State employees' median annual salary was $63,500. Local government employees earned $61,000. In the private sector, planners working for architectural and engineering firms averaged $68,200 annually. Those in scientific and technical services earned $66,300.

As in any career, work experience and accomplishments affect earnings. They also affect the level of responsibility you hold. If a transportation planner working for a local city government is hardworking, knowledgeable, and creative, he or she could in time be responsible for transportation planning for an entire state or region.

Transportation planning can be a rewarding career. It comes with a variety of responsibilities that require a broad range of skills. Some people enjoy working with other professionals to develop creative solutions to problems. Others may prefer analyzing and interpreting data. Some planners like the face-to-face meetings with city officials and the public to learn about their transportation needs and hear reactions to the proposals.

One thing that appeals to all transportation planners is how they can make people's lives more enjoyable by helping systems and facilities to grow and prosper. Are you up to the challenge?

21ST CENTURY CONTENT

Transportation planners use the term *model* to refer to mathematical equations that represent how, where, and when people choose to travel. People make travel decisions based on family needs, personal wishes, and the available routes and forms of transportation. Mathematical relationships are used to represent human behavior in making these choices. Models are important because they help estimate how much a transportation system is used. That information helps planners forecast future travel patterns and make decisions about whether to improve or build facilities to meet those needs.

SOME WELL-KNOWN TRANSPORTATION PLANNERS

Hippodamus of Miletus (498 BCE–408 BCE) was an ancient Greek architect. Known as the father of urban planning, he developed the grid plan of city layouts. Streets ran at right angles to each other. His grid plan created an order and regularity to the flow of people and goods. This was an improvement over the irregular and complex street layouts of cities of that time.

Pierre Charles L'Enfant (1754–1825) was a French-born American architect. He was responsible for designing the layout of the streets of Washington, D.C. He was personally appointed by the first U.S. president, George Washington, to design the young nation's new capital city.

Robert Moses (1888–1981) is considered the 20th-century master builder of New York City and its surrounding areas. His decisions favoring automobiles and highway systems over public transit angered many people. Yet these decisions led to the development of modern suburbs in the region. Under his leadership, New York City built many high-speed roads and **parkways**. Several major bridges and tunnels were also constructed.

GLOSSARY

aviation (ay-vee-AY-shuhn) the designing, building, and flying of aircraft

carpool (KAR-pool) to travel in a group that takes turns driving

computer simulations (kuhm-PYOO-tur sim-yuh-LAY-shuhnz) information generated by computers and based on models

freight (FRAYT) goods that are carried by train, ship, plane, or truck

models (MAH-dulz) mathematical equations that are used to represent situations, such as how, where, and when people choose to travel

monorail (MAH-nuh-rayl) a railroad that runs on one track, usually high above the ground, with the train hanging from or balanced on it

parkways (PAHRK-wayz) wide highways with grass, bushes, trees, and flowers planted in certain areas

pedestrians (puh-DESS-tree-uhnz) people traveling on foot

private sector (PRYE-vit SEK-tur) the part of the economy made up of businesses

transit (TRAN-zit) a system for carrying people or goods from one place to another, usually on trains, buses, or other vehicles

transportation (trans-pur-TAY-shuhn) a means or system for moving people and freight from one place to another

urban (UR-buhn) having to do with a city

FOR MORE INFORMATION

BOOKS

Bowden, Rob. *Transportation: Our Impact on the Planet*. Chicago: Raintree, 2004.

Careers in Focus: Transportation. New York: Ferguson Publishing Company, 2007.

Santella, Andrew. *Building the New York Subway*. New York: Children's Press, 2007.

WEB SITES

Bureau of Labor Statistics—Occupational Outlook Handbook: Urban and Regional Planners
www.bls.gov/ooh/life-physical-and-social-science/urban -and-regional-planners.htm
Get the quick facts on what planners do, where they work, and how to become a planner.

Science Buddies—Science Careers: Transportation Planner
www.sciencebuddies.org/science-fair-projects/science -engineering-careers/EnvEng_transportationplanner_c001.shtml
Learn more about what transportation planners do and what qualifications are required.

INDEX

ABOUT THE AUTHOR

Nel Yomtov is an award-winning author of nonfiction books and graphic novels for young readers. He lives in the New York City area.